THE V... KIND OF SHIRTS

'99

MARK REYNOLDS is a roving midfielder/substitute for
Dynamo Digbeth, a Sunday morning football team in
London with ever-decreasing connections to Birmingham
(excepting his own allegiance to Aston Villa).
On weekdays he is a freelance copywriter and graphic
designer. This is his fourth book.

'Wonderfully funny football quotes and gaffes. This is
a perfect Christmas stocking filler.'
Sunday Mirror

'This is a great collection of football quotes from managers,
players and fans. From the hilariously funny to the jaw-droppingly
stupid, *The Wrong Kind of Shirts* is a handy little book which
is great to dip into.'
Shoot

'There's never a shortage of football folk ready to talk
complete rubbish, and most find their way into this collection.
A good value stocking filler.'
Football365

'Even the most dedicated football fan will (find it hard to raise a smile
... It is a book with no redeeming qualities whatsoever and under no circumstances
should anyone even) consider buying it.'
Lochaber News

THE WRONG
KIND OF SHIRTS '99

compiled by
MARK REYNOLDS

illustrations by
Ian Cunliffe

FOURTH ESTATE • *London*

First published in Great Britain in 1999 by
Fourth Estate Limited
6 Salem Road
London W2 4BU
www.4thestate.co.uk

A catalogue record for this book is available from the British Library

ISBN 1–84115–190–4

1 3 5 7 9 8 6 4 2

Typeset by the author

Printed in Great Britain by
Clays Ltd, St Ives plc

For B.S., book reviewer for the
Highland News Group.
Sorry there are no Steve Patterson*
gags this year!

*Note to subs: pls chk spelling – M.R.

Introduction

Any review of a football season is necessarily subjective, and as a London-based Aston Villa supporter I may well have missed out on some top action while I was traversing the country watching my team self-destruct after leading the Premiership for four months. I therefore apologise if any of your own favourite rants, gaffes or altercations haven't made it into print in this latest collection – but at least you too have your memories.

A final reading of these pages before passing them on for publication made me realise there are at least two glaring omissions on my part: Charlton's heroic failure to stay in the Premiership for more than a season, and Birmingham City's defeat in the play-off semi-finals, both somehow eluded my ironic gaze. Charlton fans should rest easy in the knowledge that they have a manager and squad that are above such low rebuke. As for the other lot, I shall watch the current season unravel wishing with all my heart that it were they, and not Watford, suffering ten months of unending hardship in the top flight.

Before you read on (though you can skip this bit if you prefer), I'd like to thank the following for their continuing support: Clive, Stephen and the sales team at Fourth Estate; my Mum and Dad for forcing my previous books on their unsuspecting neighbours in the Midlands (sorry about the rude cover this year); Ian for another run of ace cartoons at short notice; and Farhana, Jack, Archie and my toy monkey Thelonius, for making the bits between the football more pleasurable.

Mark Reynolds, August 1999

Contents

The Greatest Football Team
in the World, Ever

'I'm starting to paint my players as gods of the game.
It's like a bus and we're going to the next stop.
If someone gets left behind, it's their own fault.'
*Alex Ferguson is incomprehensible with joy as
Manchester United clinch the championship*

'I can't believe it. I can't believe it. Bloody hell, football
... I haven't said anything to my players yet, I've just
slobbered all over them.'
*Fergie puts a further case for outlawing the immediate
post-match interview, as United win the European Cup
with two inconceivably late goals*

'Man United had to take some risks by playing three strikers, but before that they were crap. That's football, but it was crap.'
Ruud Gullit sums up the opening 89 minutes of the European Cup final

'Matt Busby would have been 90 yesterday. It must have been Dick Turpin's birthday as well.'
Alex Stepney proves that even ex-Reds can be objective

'Tonight it was not the best team that won but the luckiest. It's bitter, sad and unbelievable. We're all disappointed. You can't blame the team. We had the match in control for 90 minutes. We had bad luck, hitting the post and the crossbar. What happened afterwards is simply inexplicable.'
Bayern Munich skipper Lothar Matthäus

'I wish I'd done the lottery. The way things were going for me, I would have won anything that week.'
Teddy Sheringham gets a bit greedy

'Fergie could have saved us a lot of anguish by putting Teddy on earlier.'
Sheringham's dad Paul stretches a point

'The whole country, no matter what team they support, is absolutely thrilled. It's a fantastic achievement and an incredible finish. We're truly proud of Manchester United.'
Tony Blair speaks for the nation

'Why do two lucky injury time goals in Barcelona, an FA Cup win over the most feeble finalists in living memory and a championship win by one point make Manchester United the greatest English team of all time? The press coverage has been incredible, as has the idea that the whole country was behind them. They're an arrogant, plasticised club of mercenary morons who sum up everything appalling about modern football. I'm sick, sick, sick of it all.'
Letter to the Observer

'Manchester United are being described as being a member of European football's "elite". United fans should realise that their team has just gone from winning the European Cup as many times as Aston Villa, to winning the European Cup as many times as Nottingham Forest. "Elite" my arse.'
Letter to When Saturday Comes

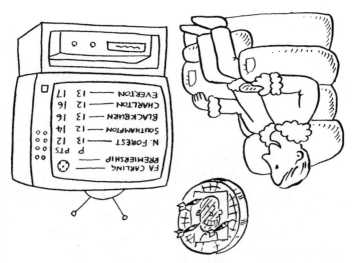

'In the house of Bassett, the television is upside-down.'
Pierre van Hooijdonk

Revolting

'I'm not prepared to let my career go down the pan.
Right now the team is not good enough to survive in
the Premiership.'
Pierre van Hooijdonk goes on strike at Forest

'He (van Hooijdonk) won't be welcome in the dressing
room. All the players are disgusted by his actions.'
*Steve Stone speaks out on behalf of the remaining
Forest squad*

'If we go down, I'll be off.'
Steve Stone undermines his argument against Big Pierre

'If someone gives me an olive branch, I'll stick it
up his arse.'
Dave Bassett rejects van Hooijdonk's call for a truce

'Joe Kinnear would have to be locked up if someone did
that here. He would have shot the person, run him over
or something drastic like that – he's very expressive.'
*Marcus Gayle warns against a van Hooijdonk-style
rebellion at Wimbledon*

'If Cloughie was van Hooijdonk's manager, he'd be
suspended – from a roof beam ... and he'd have got
Larry Lloyd and Kenny Burns to sort him out.'
*Ron Atkinson gives some advice to Bassett about dealing
with stroppy Dutchmen – five months before inheriting
the problem for himself*

'I feel that Forest is too weak for the Premier League
but my statements were regarded by many people as
arrogant. But I think their performance this season has
proved me right ... I walked out of the club because
I had to maintain my dignity.'
Van Hooijdonk insists he has acted with honour

'Can you imagine George Graham, a corrupt man who has put transfer money in his own pocket, criticising me over my behaviour? It is incredible.'
Van Hooijdonk hits back at a surprisingly vociferous critic

'I'm gobsmacked by the whole issue and find it hard to accept. I find it difficult to understand how anyone in Stan's position, with the talent and money he has, is stressed. Stress has always been around, but I thought it related more to a 29-year-old at Rochdale with a mortgage and three children who had only three months left on his contract.'
John Gregory appears to doubt Stan Collymore's sincerity as the player books in for stress counselling

'It's strange that Stan Collymore is being treated for stress. When I was his manager, it was me who had all the stress.'
Frank Clark

'I'm sure Stan will do very well indeed in the First Division. You only have to look at his record – he has always done well and scored goals in the lower divisions.'
John Gregory packs Collymore off to Fulham with faint praise

THE WRONG KIND OF SHIRTS '99

'I am not going back. I feel let down by the club and I am unhappy about the whole situation. I have done nothing wrong yet I have been fined two weeks' wages.'
Dietmar Hamann can't work out why he is unable to walk away from Newcastle a few months into his contract

'I am clear in my mind I will still be in England next season and wearing an Arsenal shirt.'
Nicolas Anelka states his unambiguous intentions as Arsenal jostle for the title

'I don't intend to remain at Arsenal. My preference would be to join Marseille, but I may go to Italy or Spain.'
Anelka is struck by homesickness at the season's close

'I don't want to go to Italy just yet – it's too early. It is true that I would like to play in Marseille. If they really want me, let them prove it to me.'
Anelka waits for Marseille's call

'I hope one day to play in Spain. I would love to walk out at the Nou Camp wearing the colours of Barcelona.'
Catalunya takes Anelka's fancy

'Wenger thinks it would be bad for me to go to Real,
but it's Spain or nothing. Italy doesn't interest me.
I don't like their game.'
Anelka announces he's off to Madrid ...

'My priority is still to play for Real Madrid, but if that
cannot be possible then why not go to Lazio? I prefer
to go there than to stay with Arsenal.'
... but deigns to consider Rome ...

'It's Lazio that interests me now. It's a very big club.
I am not going to Juventus. It's Lazio or nothing.'
... when Lazio offer to pay him around £80,000 a week

'Get shot of him, Arsène – he's just a spoilt Frog.'
*A Sun readers' poll elicits some helpful advice on how
Monsieur Wenger should deal with his compatriot*

'It has always been Arsenal's wish to retain the services
of Nicolas Anelka. With the season less than two weeks
away ... the club has withdrawn the possibility of the
player departing and expect him to resume full training.'
*David Dein is curiously optimistic about
retaining the player*

'It's comical. I think they'll be waiting for me for a long time. This break from soccer will be good for me.'
Anelka

'Nicolas has a lot of talent but is by no means the finished article. Sure, he has pace but he can't head a ball.'
Arsenal reserve team coach George Armstrong puts the £23 million transfer wrangle in perspective

'I couldn't care less about him. I had forgotten about Anelka. It will be interesting to see if he plays in our first team.'
Ray Parlour

'The last thing you should do is criticise your teammates.'
Saint Pierre van Hooijdonk points out where Anelka went wrong

Cultural Exchanges

'We don't have this narrow view at this club that
players have to be English, Scottish or Irish.'
Chelsea managing director Colin Hutchinson offers up
a surprise revelation

'Some foreigners come to England and adapting is
very difficult, it's a big change. But Argentinians
can go anywhere.'
Eminent import Gustavo di Lella is as good as his word
as he signs for Hartlepool

'We're all members of the European Union now.
So if you're a Portuguese window cleaner, you can
come and clean windows in London. If you're a
Portuguese footballer, ditto.'
David Mellor

'As soon as I got off the plane and felt the sun on my face I thought, "Yep, this'll do for me."'
Ron Atkinson considers taking charge of the South African national team

'I've a Portuguese phrasebook at home, but I haven't read it yet.'
Graeme Souness takes his time acclimatising at Benfica

'When the Italians tell me it's pasta on the plate, I check under the sauce to make sure that it is ... (I expect) scheming, diving and ref-baiting.'
Alex Ferguson sets the scene for the European Cup quarter-final against Internazionale

'I've always believed in the English sense of fair play. But Alex Ferguson is Scottish and apparently they have no sense of fair play in Scotland.'
Inter coach Mercea Lucescu hits back

'I used to have a good opinion of English football. Now I think it's total crap.'
Lens' Tony Vareilles rules out an immediate move to the Premiership after his controversial dismissal against Arsenal

'I've just had enough and I won't change my mind.
I'm totally fed up with what has been happening.
I've been sent off as many times as Dennis Wise.
I'll leave it to other people to decide who deserves
their red cards more.'
Emmanuel Petit threatens to quit the Premiership

'I'm fed up with the English way of life, the lack of sun,
the whole business. I haven't talked to the media for
three months, yet every day I find myself in the papers.
I don't think it's Emmanuel Petit who's the problem,
I just think that the French stir things up in England.
We won the World Cup, I won the title with Arsenal,
and we beat England at Wembley. I think the French in
general simply bother the English.'
Petit breaks his media embargo to speak to L'Equipe *about
how the English view the French as boastful and aloof*

'I have never said I was ready to leave Arsenal and
English football. Why would I?'
Petit suffers a memory lapse

'I've joined West Ham and I don't care about any other clubs. I want to show what I can do here and I'm not interested in moving on.'
Javier Margas seems unperturbed at a lack of first-team outings

'I have spoken a lot with my family and what is for sure is that none of us is happy with life in England. If I am not playing in Chile, I would rather not play any more.'
Margas has a change of heart after going AWOL from the club

'When Gullit came I was dropped into the reserves without any explanation. Then, when I approached him in the dressing room, he only talked to me in English.'
Alessandro Pistone has communication difficulties

'People here think Australia is just like *Neighbours* and *Home & Away*. I don't know where they got that idea from.'
Harry Kewell

'For every foreigner, I would say learn the language – unless you come to Chelsea, perhaps.'
Dan Petrescu

'I wouldn't care if all eleven came from Mars, as long
as they're wearing Chelsea blue and playing their
heart out for the club.'
Tony Banks

'The J-League has many important players, but lacks creativity and personality on the field. Once, a player fouled me and then followed me around the field for a good five minutes, apologising ... The Japanese are far too nice. Football is for men.'
Hristo Stoichkov

'I'd like there to be more Spaniards in the side so they can understand you when you speak.'
Barcelona stopper Sergi tires of Louis Van Gaal's Dutch-only recruitment policy

'Didi was popular among the lads. During the Christmas party he was given a copy of *Mein Kampf* as a joke present and he took it well. He seemed to warm to us after that.'
Anonymous Newcastle United player explains how his colleagues tried to make Dietmar Hamann feel at home

'I seldom played for them, because I didn't want to. I felt ill and I was desperate to leave. The weather over there was bad. It was so horrible I spent every day shut up indoors at home.'
Mikael Madar swaps the blue half of Merseyside for sunny Paris

'I miss the people. I miss the smell of the pine trees. I miss living outside. Here, you live inside ... My mother says to me: "How is the weather?" and I say: "Awful." So she says: "David, you must always keep some sunshine in your mind. And we are waiting for you." They are all waiting for me. For the little prince to return to his village.'
David Ginola

'The sun I see in Rome I never saw in London.
It nearly always rains.'
Attilio Lombardo

'I'm cool and relaxed. I've a Scottish mentality,
not a Latin one.'
*Graeme Souness, about to be sacked at Benfica, decides to
get his insults in first*

'There's no chance of an English girl winning Miss
World ... the meal I had in my hotel was disgusting,
I was sick afterwards. Their food isn't fit for hamsters.'
Silvio Maric settles in at Newcastle

'The English players like to feel superior to us. You see
it in their eyes, in the dressing room and on the pitch.
It is in their nature.'
*Nicolas Anelka gees himself up (rather successfully, as it
turns out) for France's friendly at Wembley*

'The food wasn't what I am used to.'
*Celtic's Darren Jackson pines for neeps and tatties during
a brief trial with China's Dalian Wanda*

Getting Along

'Have you ever thought it might be you?'
*Alan Shearer's alleged mild rebuke to Glenn Hoddle in the
Luxembourg dressing room*

'The manager took me out on my own and put me
through the hardest running I have ever done. I was
absolutely shattered. Then he took me into his office and
told me, "You're sold." I was laughing, I couldn't believe it.
I asked him why he put me through that and he said,
"I wanted you to have something to remember me by."'
*Keith O'Neill offers a glimpse of Bruce Rioch's
man-management technique*

'The Arsenal players are belligerent and like a scrap
... they turn games into a battle to try to make the
opposition lose concentration.'
Alex Ferguson

'It's not my policy to criticise other teams like this.
I was stitched up and I feel I have been betrayed
– the conversation was off the record.'
*Alex Ferguson denies intending to criticise Arsenal players
– at least in public*

'Two players think they can turn performances on and
off like a tap, but it doesn't work like that. At this level
you can say goodbye to that fancy dan rubbish.
Good players are not embarrassed to work and come
off looking knackered.'
*Sheffield Wednesday boss Danny Wilson refuses to
single out Paolo di Canio and Benito Carbone for their
lack of workrate*

'Football is the only job I know where you can turn up,
do a dreadful job, and demand to be paid in full.'
*Scarborough chairman John Russell berates his players
after a 5–1 thrashing by Cambridge United*

'Dick Knight wouldn't recognise Gareth Barry if he
stood on Brighton beach in an Albion shirt with a ball
tucked under his arm and a seagull on his head.'
*John Gregory hits back at the Brighton chairman's
compensation claim*

'When we bought him we did not buy a striker, we bought a black cannibal who calls himself a striker.'
Trabzonspor president Mehmet Ali Yilmaz inadvertently causes offence to Kevin Campbell on Turkish TV

'I'd like to be really popular, but I don't think it's going to happen no more.'
David Beckham faces up to reality

'Defenders should know by now that they must stay on their feet against a player of Ginola's ability.'
George Graham rather misses the point as Barnsley's John Hendrie becomes the latest boss to accuse Ginola of diving

'I want to stay but things have to be right. If the club can ask £10 million for me then they have got to pay for £10 million-worth of player. Is there anybody else at the club worth £10 million?'
Jimmy Floyd Hasselbaink

'I took a step backwards when I left AC Milan for Chelsea. Four years ago, who had heard of Chelsea?'
Marcel Desailly

'What? Overjoyed? No, it was awful. Awful. They stole my dream ... Why? WHY?'
David Ginola relives France's World Cup win

'We are not going to appoint another unproven manager, and we are not going to approach someone who has reached the end of the line.'
Sheffield United chairman Mike McDonald refutes media claims that he's about to appoint Bobby Gould

'It's getting very normal for players to say "my wife can't settle, I've got to go". It's the biggest load of Betty Swollocks.'
Mark Lawrenson

'The move was forced on me. I was numb with shock. It sickened me, I couldn't believe it. I wanted to finish my career at Everton.'
Duncan Ferguson endears himself to the Geordies

'Two weeks ago, Dwight openly stated to me that he wanted to play for Manchester United. That really hurt me, and if I had had a gun, I would have shot him.'
John Gregory has a pop at Yorkie

'I would ask every fan to think what they would do if they were offered another job which they would really like to do.'
Dwight Yorke fails to realise that he's just given up every Villa fan's dream employment

'I'm outraged at the way this was done. I don't need a job that badly that I'll let people walk all over me.'
Harry Redknapp objects to the West Ham board's sale of Andy Impey to Leicester

'The books have to be balanced and Harry knows that as well as I did. He can like it or lump it.'
West Ham managing director Peter Storrie strikes a blow for board power

'He (Overmars) plays only for himself and will never give me a ball I can score from. There's no reason I should stay quiet and run like a dog behind the missiles he sends my way.'
Nicolas Anelka

'He's sent in more sick notes than Darren Anderton.'
Danny Wilson loses patience with Paolo di Canio

'Ken Bates has been quoted as saying that we're just a club from the slum side of Manchester. To me, Chelsea could move their stadium to the middle of Harrods and win 15 championships on the trot, and even if you moved Old Trafford to Beirut they still wouldn't be as big as us.'
Gary Neville

'Around 50 per cent of Nationwide managers do not have the right qualities. They're there on the old pro network ... They wouldn't have a clue if I asked them about a player's cardiovascular respiratory system or his capability to dilute lactic acid.'
Michael Knighton explains why he makes the perfect team boss

'Journalists can make a sane, semi-intelligent, rational, straightforward, non-eccentric reasonable person come across as a raving bloody lunatic.'
Michael Knighton concedes that he may have given the press a little too much to work with

'I don't give a toss if he's unhappy. This is a team game.'
John Gregory gives Paul Merson the benefit of his advice

'If he keeps saying these things about me in public, we'll fall out.'
Merse plays Gregory at his own game

'We've got a massive game on Saturday, Cheltenham at home, and I have to take action.'
Lincoln City chairman John Reames explains his decision to sack the management team and take charge of footballing affairs

'If he ever decides to sack himself, there's a job for him on Hackney marshes – I've never seen anyone move the goalposts as quickly or as fast as he did.'
Ex-Lincoln coach Wally Downes

'Everyone deserves five, six or seven chances, but after 77 you blot your copybook.'
Martin O'Neill drops Frank Sinclair from Leicester's Worthington Cup final squad

'A lot of my players are rubber dinghy men. The ship is going down, and they say they'll go for help.'
Brian Kidd's titanic struggle continues as Blackburn slump to a 2–1 defeat at home to relegated Forest

'I've got a gut feeling that this is the time to go.
I can no longer motivate these players.'
*Bobby Gould finally wakes up to the clamour for his
removal as Wales lose 4–0 in Italy*

'I thought I was doing quite a good job.'
*Roy Hodgson laments his sacking from
bottom-of-the-table Blackburn*

'What a draw for us – we are going to be up against
the Spice Girls.'
*Internazionale defender Fabio Galante looks forward
to facing Manchester United in the European Cup
quarter-final*

'If it's not a contract I want then I won't sign it.
That's not a threat.'
Roy Keane

'I'm convinced managers don't sign me because they
think I would be after their jobs in a couple of months.'
*Chris Waddle appears to forget his appalling record
as Burnley boss*

'I'm better known around the world than Kevin Keegan, me ... I am hands on in everything I do, my chipboard business, engineering, shipping, warehousing, recycling. Now I've got football. I've been in it two weeks and know everything there is to know about it.'
New Darlington chairman George Reynolds announces his credentials

'It will be a major test of Olsen's ability to keep it going.'
Joe Kinnear challenges his successor to continue Wimbledon's disastrous end-of-season run

'I would never have them call me "Sir" – it will still be "Boss".'
Alex Ferguson keeps things informal post-knighthood

Fair Play

'After we scored and there was a fight, I knew what
I had done. I know the rules, I know you have to give
the ball back to the opposition and I made a mistake.
I wanted to make an impression, but not like this.'
*Nwankwo Kanu apologises for his accidental
gamesmanship in the FA Cup against Sheffield United*

'It did not cross my mind when the ball was passed that
anything was wrong, but after I scored I immediately
thought "this is not good" and there was no way
I wanted to win after that.'
Marc Overmars

'Kanu is sad and there is no way Arsenal want to win games like this. It was an accident and that's why we want to replay.'
Arsène Wenger insists on the gentlemanly course of action

'We're honest, but we're not stupid.'
Wenger balks at the suggestion the tie should be replayed in Sheffield

'You know it was over the line, I know it was over the line. The only people who didn't were the referee and the linesman. I think the linesman's view was blocked by the keeper lying in the back of the net with the ball.'
Denis Smith queries a disallowed West Brom goal at Bolton

'The referee was absolute bobbins. And if you want a translation of bobbins, it's crap.'
Dave Jones

'The only time Ginola was possibly fouled was right at the end when he was tackled three yards outside the box, stumbled and then threw himself into the area. Maybe he was trying for a long-jump record.'
Joe Kinnear

'The referee has handed it to them. That's the kind of man we had tonight.'
Alex Ferguson gets nervous on the title run-in as David Elleray sends off Denis Irwin and awards Liverpool a dubious penalty, enabling them to level the score from 2–0 down

'If Arsenal or Chelsea win the Premiership by one or two points, I trust they will strike a commemorative medal for Elleray.'
Martin Edwards

'Managers have a responsibility to protect referees. You have to believe that they give their best.'
Arsène Wenger advises Alex and Martin to lay off match officials

'Maybe I don't know the rules, but I thought it was a penalty if you kill someone in the box without taking the ball.'
Wenger can't quite practise what he preaches

'I felt my performance during 120 minutes of frantic
football was good and it's just typical of a manager
to blame the referee rather than look at his own
side's shortcomings.'
*Paul Durkin responds to the criticisms of George Graham
after an eventful FA Cup semi-final*

'I saw the Barcelona president going into the referee's
dressing room afterwards. I'm sure he was pleased
to see him.'
*Alex Ferguson refuses to be drawn on the award of two
penalties to the Catalans*

'If you end up going to the hairdressers every day, by the seventh day you're going to get a haircut.'
Paul Merson takes a roundabout way to describe the temptations on offer at the Riverside

Sex, Drugs and Recreational Hazards

'Good strikers only score goals when they have had good sex the night before a match. It is completely crazy to have pre-match training camps. A footballer only thinks about one thing but instead of sharing his double room with a beautiful woman, it is with a teammate.'
Romario

'The majority of my squad are near teetotal and the players have not even had a card school for five years.'
Gazza apologist Bryan Robson disputes Paul Merson's claims of a boozing and betting culture at Middlesbrough

THE WRONG KIND OF SHIRTS '99

'If the present number of games continues, we will all have to take drugs to survive. Some players already do, I know that, but I'm not giving any names – I don't want years of drug scandals.'
Emmanuel Petit opens an intriguing debate

'Premiership players have cocaine, cannibis and all sorts of funny tablets buzzing around in their systems.'
Ron Atkinson brazenly attempts to shift a few extra copies of his latest memoir

'He's gone through a substantial rehabilitation programme and the FA and his club are protecting his anonymity in order to assist in his rehabilitation.'
Alan Hudson, the FA's head of sports medicine, safeguards the identity of a 17-year-old trainee who tested positive for heroin

'My world has fallen apart, I've been a bloody fool. I knew all about random tests but it's one of those things you think will never happen to you ...'
17-year-old trainee Anthony Parry sells a 'My Drugs Hell' piece to the Mirror *upon his release by Newcastle*

'A goalscorer does everything by instinct. When she shoved her tongue down my throat I acted instinctively and bit it.'
Barry Town striker Chris Pike pleads an unlikely defence after biting his wife's tongue at a dinner party

'I am not and have never been a bigot.'
Craig Brown insists that any anti-Catholic songs he may or may not have sung into an ex-girlfriend's answerphone could only have been meant in jest

'If I rescued a toddler from a burning building, certain elements of the press would portray me as a child molester.'
Craig's brother Jock reflects on the family's relations with the tabloids

'Shall we say, in football parlance, he isn't over the moon.'
Detective Chief Inspector John Davis announces Roy Keane's arrest for alleged assault on two women in a Manchester nightclub

'People are really missing why I did this book. This is about alcoholism, my disease. Two years ago I was dead.'
Tony Adams describes his remarkable rehabilitation

'Tony (Adams) is having piano lessons, and when he's
not thinking about his piano, he's writing poems.
We are like two old dears.'
Ray Parlour on the perils of giving up the booze

'There is no bloody way we are getting involved in corrupt behaviour. We will come down like a ton of bricks on any country who does that in the bidding for the 2006 finals.'
Tony Banks overlooks the small matter of the FA's £3 million 'unconditional' loan to the FAW that did for Graham Kelly and Ken Wiseman

'Dwight made Andy look small in comparison and was far more in control.'
Nicky Kilroy, 18, delights News of the World *readers with tales of her three-in-a-bed love romps*

'Dwight told me he had only two friends in Manchester – Andy Cole and his toy monkey. He called it Brian.'
... or is that four-in-a-bed?

'It was bad enough her sleeping with someone else, but going off with two men, and United players at that, is the lowest of the low.'
Nicky's ex Mark Glynn, a Man City fan

'He's the most beautiful person I've ever met.'
Aussie soap star Emily Symons gushes over her sex-god fiancé Matt le Tissier

'Big? It's magnificent!'
Alex Ferguson confesses he's still in awe of Dion Dublin's
natural gifts

'It's a very bad injury, quite terrible. I can't go into detail
but there was blood coming from his penis, which was
obviously frightening for the lad.'
Gerry Francis goes into unnecessary detail about an
injury to Antti Heinola

'He was pretending to graze like a sheep – it's a goal
celebration he picked up from Rigobert Song.'
Gerard Houllier implausibly vindicates Robbie Fowler's
cocaine-sniffing gag at Everton

'He has done a lot of work for us at grassroots level.'
A Nike spokesman sticks by Fowler

Handbags

'Verbals between players are part and parcel of the game. Always have been, always will be. You can't take it out of the game.'
Dave Bassett

'Come on, come on. Give it to me up the arse.'
Robbie Fowler (allegedly) indulges in some very particular verbals aimed at Graeme Le Saux

'All is fair in love, war and football. Graeme has to accept he is going to get this kind of abuse and live with it. The moment he reacts he has lost. True winners learn to rise above it.'
Gianluca Vialli takes a surprisingly equable view of Fowler's homophobic attack

'Nobody cares if Le Saux is gay or not. It is the fact that he openly reads the *Guardian* that makes him the most reviled man in football.'
Mirror editor and reviled journalist Piers Morgan

'Your report shows Robbie Fowler's actions in a new light. I had assumed his gestures to mean "Look at me, I'm an arsehole", an assessment with which it would be hard to disagree.'
Letter to Graeme Le Saux's favourite newspaper

'The incident in which I was elbowed in the back of the head was highly regrettable. Graeme may have misinterpreted my actions, which were not intended to cause any offence, and it is unfortunate that attempts have been made since the game by others to make me the scapegoat for what took place.'
Robbie Fowler issues a less than fulsome apology

'It's funny, throughout my career I've been described
as "cerebral", but I had to look that word up
in a dictionary.'
Graeme Le Saux tries to convince Hello! *readers he's
just as thick as the next footballer*

'I gave him a shove, but it was hardly done with much
force. He took three or four steps before falling over
in a strange way – like someone diving for a penalty.
In fact it was so odd he would probably have been given
a yellow card if he had been a player. To me it looked
like someone who was acting.'
Paolo di Canio defends his assault on ref Paul Alcock

'Eyal (Berkovic) is a match-winner who makes about
90 per cent of our goals. He only weighs nine stone but
people can't get near him, not even just to kick him.'
*Harry Redknapp puts the John Hartson training ground
incident behind him*

Fans' Notes

'All fans love to see a complete lunatic on the pitch and that's what we've got with di Canio. West Ham have traded a player who kicks teammates in the head for a player who attacks referees. I don't know if that's progress.'
On a Mission fanzine editor Shane Barber welcomes the white-booted wonder

'Replacing your home – difficult to do. Replacing your family – impossible. Leaving your job – easy.'
The alarming message attached to an unlit petrol bomb delivered to the home of Luton chairman David Kohler

'I'd heard the Pope was a Fulham fan so, as it was Easter, I thought I'd give him a ring to try and get a good-luck message. But I couldn't believe it when I actually got through to this press spokesman at the Vatican – he knew who we were playing at the weekend.'
Fulham Independent Fanline operator Ken Myers tracks down the ultimate celebrity fan

'There were parents bringing their kids to matches and encouraging them to shout abuse at me. It's pathetic.'
Steve McMahon explains his decision to resign as Swindon manager

'I have decided to leave the England Members' Club. I'm simply not prepared to watch a match surrounded by complete morons.'
Ex-Labour spin doctor Charlie Whelan vows to stick to watching Spurs with the singular Richard Littlejohn

'When you lose a game in Germany you lock yourself in, afraid of fans who would beat you up. In Barnsley you are drunk after 30 minutes because everyone wants to buy you a beer to console you.'
Barnsley keeper Lars Leese

'I had a brief moment of panic because I was covered in tomato ketchup and I thought it was blood.'
Ref Paul Durkin relives his close encounter with a hot dog thrown from the stands at Oldham

'I don't think it was an unpleasant atmosphere. I have always said Scottish supporters are excellent, so why should I change this view now?'
Jozef Venglos, in denial after a trouble-strewn Old Firm derby

'Imagine putting yourself through all that nonsense for £250? Or £251 if you count tips? ... (referee) Hugh Dallas probably still can't believe he was struck by a pound coin while doing his job. Where did a Celtic fan get that kind of money?'
The Daily Record's ace columnist Tam Cowan takes a stern view of the crowd disturbance

'Stéphane Mahé has been blamed for starting all the trouble and it's difficult to argue with that. His refusal to leave the pitch after being red-carded was a disgrace but hardly surprising. Well, you know what it's like trying to get a Frenchman into a bath.'
Cowan finds a still wider group of people to disparage

'When I got back to my car on Saturday a window had been smashed for the third time. I drove home down the M4, rain pouring in and feeling miserable as sin. I thought to myself, "Someone is trying to tell me something here."'
Ray Harford sees the writing on the wall at QPR

'In the light of recent events, I feel that Lee may not have the fans' full backing.'
Peter Reid transfer-lists Lee Clark, judging that wearing a 'sad Mackem bastards' t-shirt in public could meet with criticism on Wearside

'Sex and chocolate aren't as good as football.'
Sunderland fans indulge in a spot of male bonding

'You can stick George Graham up your arse.'
Tottenham fans acknowledge the club's approach to the ex-Arsenal boss

'Man in a raincoat's blue-and-white army.'
Spurs fans refuse to sing George Graham's name even after his appointment as manager

'Niall Quinn's disco pants are the best,
They go from his arse to his vest,
They're better than Adam and the Ants,
Niall Quinn's disco pants.'
Those wacky Sunderland fans

'We're shit, but Wales are worse.'
*Northern Ireland fans find solace as Turkey race to
a three-goal lead against their heroes*

'He's blond, he's quick,
His name's a porno flick,
Emmanuel, Emmanuel.'
Arsenal fans

'You're not famous any more.'
Derby fans celebrate Liverpool's demise

Ho, Ho, Ho

'I have lost some money buying club shares but at least I can go to shareholders' meetings and criticise myself.'
Martin O'Neill

'Of course we're going to take the Old Trafford game seriously. We will be naming José Dominguez as our substitute goalkeeper.'
George Graham asserts he will do everything in his power to help Arsenal win the title (José Dominguez is 5' 3")

Des Lynam: Sheffield Wednesday are a bit erratic, aren't they?
Mark Lawrenson: They can be, yes.

THE WRONG KIND OF SHIRTS '99

'Cyril the Swan was a mere cygnet when Swansea
last had a night like this.'
*Peter Drury watches the Swansea mascot celebrate FA Cup
victory over West Ham*

'Trevor Brooking, Geoff Hurst, Bobby Moore,
Lorraine Chase, Alf Garnett, David Essex,
Pauline Fowler, Harry Redknapp, do you hear me?
Your boys took one hell of a beating.'
Swansea's Clubcall line

'It's a pleasure to be standing up here ... It's a pleasure to
be standing up.'
*George Best accepts the Football Hall of Fame's Footballer
of the Century award with customary self-parody*

'He (Lee Mills) is the best attacker of the ball in the
air in the division. But that is probably down to his
lack of brains.'
*Port Vale midfielder Stuart Talbot extols the club's
star striker*

'That was a Kate Moss cross – it was a little behind.'
Mark Lawrenson

'I made friends with Alan on my first day at Ibrox.
I walked into the dressing room and made a point
of sitting beside him because he was the only guy there
who looked fatter than me. I reckoned if I hung about
with him, I would look good in comparison, so we
became mates.'
*Paul Gascoigne pays tribute to Alan McLaren at his former
colleague's testimonial*

'I'll tell you what, that Yorke and Cole are good enough
to get in our team.'
*Ron Atkinson makes light of Forest's 8–1 reverse at home
to Manchester United*

'It was a brilliant result considering we never kicked a
ball for 90 minutes.'
*Dundee's Jim McInally muses on an improbable 1–1 draw
with St Johnstone*

'I started at the bottom in 1974 – and I'm still there.'
*Stenhousemuir's 43-year-old stopper Graeme Armstrong
notches up a British record 864 league appearances*

'My big ambition is to drive into United's training
ground behind the wheel of a Reliant Robin.'
Dwight Yorke vows to give the Ferrari a day off

'There you have it, ladies and gentlemen,
Radio Five Live: news, sport – and history.'
Ian Payne reports a rare Everton goal at Goodison Park

'Only sixth? I've got to be worse than that, haven't I?'
Michael Knighton takes exception to his placing in
Football365's list of the 10 worst chairmen of all time

'I believe in Methuselah, Frankenstein, alien beings,
flying saucers and the Hand of God. But most of all
I believe in on-loan goalkeepers from Swindon who
score goals in the dying seconds.'
Michael Knighton celebrates Jimmy Glass's last-day,
95th-minute winner, which keeps Carlisle in the
Football League at the expense of Scarborough

High Finance

'We will not lose our identity. No one is going to
pay that sort of money to destroy the club, not even
Rupert Murdoch.'
*Manchester United plc chairman Sir Roland Smith
defends the honour of the News International boss*

'I have to think about the pensioners who might lose
out if I don't take up the best offer.'
*Martin Edwards reaches for an onion and explains why he's
backing the BSkyB bid*

THE WRONG KIND OF SHIRTS '99

'Selling United will prove that he knows the price of
everything and the value of nothing.'
*Independent Manchester United Supporters Association
spokesman Andy Walsh clearly has no elderly relatives*

'Of course it's too much for a footballer. I've seen
shopping centres built for less.'
Jaap Stam queries his £10.5 million fee

'Ken Bates keeps telling me I'm the best bargain he's
ever had. I find that pleasing and I'm happy at Chelsea,
but I don't want to end up becoming the club cretin.
I signed a good contract when I came to the club and
I have since doubled my salary, but I hope to quadruple
it very soon ... I have always said that I am a footballer
as much for the money as for the glory.'
Frank Leboeuf

'I'm paid an extraordinary amount of money. I get
more than enough. If players don't want to come to
Arsenal on the wages I'm on, there's something
wrong with them.'
Tony Adams

'This move is certainly not for the money, although there is a lot of it.'
Steve McManaman moves to Real Madrid for footballing reasons only

'I grew up fixing my own toast, tying my own shoes, wiping my own ass, and just because I have money and I can pay someone to do it, doesn't mean I'm going to.'
Kasey Keller draws the line on personal luxuries

'I could have gone abroad and lived like a king, but I followed my heart.'
Mark Bosnich opts to slum it on around £25,000 a week at Old Trafford

'Some of them are being unreasonable and unhealthy in their demands. We have players looking for £3,000-a-week basic.'
St Johnstone chairman Geoff Brown condemns spiralling wages north of the border

'I must be the biggest mug in the world to buy this club for £23 million.'
Crystal Palace chairman Mark Goldberg finds something upon which he and Ron Noades can agree

THE WRONG KIND OF SHIRTS '99

'British players have one half-decent season then find a stupid price tag has been placed on their heads ... we intend taking a stand against unrealistic prices.'
Leeds chairman Peter Ridsdale pauses before splashing out £5 million on Sunderland's Michael Bridges

'What I cannot allow to happen is to bring in players for nine and 10 million pounds, find that they don't do it and that I've destroyed our youth policy. If that means we get into the Premiership and go lose, lose, lose, you need people around you who understand what this club is, who understand this club's place.'
Graham Taylor prepares Watford fans for an arduous season in the top flight

'If I can get Slaven (Bilic) back for nothing it will be great business. Even if he costs us £1 million he will be worth it.'
Harry Redknapp makes light of a £3.5 million-plus devaluation in the player he sold to Everton two years ago

'Anybody who's spending over 100 per cent of their income on wages is paying more than they should.'
Deloitte & Touche financial wizard Ian Burton has alarming news for club chairmen

'I have a soft spot for Blackburn, I must admit. It's to do with a common proclivity for throwing money about and never spotting a bargain. Jack Walker and I should never go shopping together, that's for sure.'
Times *columnist Lynn Truss*

'All of you will appreciate the irony that a club like ours now has the cheek, confidence and wit to stride out with "Skint" on its shirts. This deal is typical of the new spirit at the Albion.'
Brighton chairman Dick Knight announces a new sponsorship deal with a local record label

'I came in one particular morning, I didn't have my chairman, I didn't have anyone on the board as such, and a couple of men in grey suits came in with a machine gun and they just shot who they wanted.'
Alan Ball exaggerates the methods of Portsmouth's receivers

'I sat there on deadline day and watched the comings and goings on Ceefax. It got to five o'clock and I thought I'd lost two or three players. Then I phoned the chairman and he said I'd lost five.'
Palace boss Steve Coppell watches on helplessly as the administrators trim his playing staff

'We're not impressed (with Uefa's plans). We're stuck with Media Partners because they're offering more money, end of story.'
Real Madrid president Lorenzo Sanz reveals the secret formula for revamping the Champions' League

'Manchester United is the football brand on everyone's lips. A treble-winning side enhances dramatically the exposure and potential of the club.'
Man United director Peter Kenyon takes a shareholder's pride in a successful season

'People used to want to beat us because we were the Premiership champions. Now it will be because we are European Cup holders – and if we win in Brazil we'll be champions of the universe.'
Alex Ferguson refuses to settle for mere world domination

'This is the end result of an addiction to greed, prestige and personal ambition. And amid it all there has been a remarkable snub to the people who matter most in these things ... the fans.'
Andy Gray criticises Man United's FA Cup withdrawal in favour of the moneyspinning World Team Championship

'I am sure you would not wish your supporters to be left with the impression that Manchester United considers the FA Cup to be of little importance compared to the financial advantages of building a global brand.'
Shadow Sport Secretary Peter Ainsworth in a letter to Martin Edwards

'Fans of Manchester United don't give a damn about England's national team, so all this talk about us representing our country is nonsense.'
IMUSA spokesman

'Manchester United should be playing in the FA Cup. I am amazed that they have treated their supporters in such a shabby way.'
Kate Hoey steps into Tony Banks's size tens as Sports Minister

'Going to play in Brazil will be a hard challenge for us. The next game after we come back is against Arsenal in the league. The Arsenal fans in government who are trying to get us back in the FA Cup should think about that.'
Alex Ferguson

'The knowledge of the ordinary Chinese supporter about our club is quite staggering. Already there is a massive fan base ... and when you think there are 1.2 billion people in this vast country, so much can be achieved.'
Peter Kenyon indulges his daydreams on Man United's Far East tour

'Poverty among fans is grossly exaggerated when you see what they spend elsewhere. A small minority are poor and can't afford it.'
Ken Bates defends his latest ticket price hike

'The average working lad can't understand or relate to the money involved in the game, but he'll go along with it if he believes it will make his team better.'
Alex Ferguson joins Bates in patronising the masses

'I was advised there could be serious difficulties with me having a controlling interest in both clubs if we were in the same European tournament.'
Rangers chairman David Murray finds an improbable obstacle to a proposed buyout of Manchester City

'We hope to turn this club into the Macclesfield Town of the south.'
Rodney Marsh announces his impressive ambitions for Ashford Town

Tactics

'Last night I was lying in bed with the missus and she said, "Harry, if you're drawing, push Trevor Sinclair up front," so I gambled – and it worked a treat.'
Harry Redknapp sneaks a 1–0 win at Chelsea

'On the Monday after the match you think of changing 10 or 11 of the team. By Tuesday it's down to three or four. By Thursday, two, and by Friday you have to pick the same bastards as last week.'
John Toshack bemoans the limited playing resources at Real Madrid

'I've been brought in to give a kick up the backside to a lot of players.'
Phil Thompson outlines his specialist duties as Liverpool's assistant manager

'In a one-on-one situation, Dad told me to stand there and shout abuse at them while they're running through. I never did that, though I did a few times after they scored.'
Jonathan Gould wisely ignores some early coaching advice from his father, Bobby

'There's nothing difficult about making football work. All you have to do is build a stadium, fill all the seats and just win every week.'
Darlington chairman George Reynolds

'I thought we created a couple of chances but it's the same old story every game for us. We don't score goals and we don't have a natural goalscorer. Hopefully, someone will turn up before our next qualifier.'
Northern Ireland boss Lawrie McMenemy prays for a miracle

'Football is a simple game. It's just that the players make it difficult.'
Gordon Strachan

'I want to get the England team playing as the England team should play – playing the sort of football the fans want to see, not what technical directors all over the world feel is the right way to play ... Too many times England have played the way they were supposed to. I will play the English way.'
Kevin Keegan trusts in the parochial, for no discernible reason

Training

'Over here you do not train the day after a match, but I am going to bring that in. I also don't think players should drink on Saturday night if they have a midweek game. One beer will do no harm but five would have a big influence.'

Egil Olsen rings the changes at Wimbledon

'The curry thing started when I went on a school trip to the local mosque in Smethwick. They offered me a taste of curry, and I've never looked back.'

Lee Hughes

'The old adage that you can't turn a donkey into a racehorse is true, but you can become a faster donkey.'
Kevin Keegan

'There aren't many centre-forwards like me any more. These days you have to be mobile, flexible, athletic.'
Bob Latchford recalls the golden age of the lumbering striker

'Trailing round the shops with your missus for three hours can wear you out. I've told the lads they have to get their feet up when they get home. I don't want them lugging bags of shopping around days before a game.'
New Swindon boss Jimmy Quinn gets the little ladies onside

'When we scored hat-tricks we used to get a crate of whisky. I scored four hat-tricks that year, so I got 48 bottles in all, which I distributed among the lads. No wonder we got relegated.'
Bob Hatton recalls player bonuses, seventies-style

'In the first few weeks of pre-season training, you just sweat out the alcohol.'
Jokerit coach Pasi Rautianien excuses West Ham's slow start to their InterToto campaign

'Ron was a great person to work for and he will shake things up at Forest ... I always liked a pint of beer and he would make sure he put one on my table whenever we were at hotels on a Friday night before games, even if I didn't ask for one.'
Garry Birtles describes Mr Atkinson's motivation skills

'I have been lazy and I will be lazy after football. If I just had to answer to myself I would just go down to the south of France and be one lazy bastard. But I am a working man. I work my butt off every training session, maybe more than the other players ... My fitness has improved so much that, before a game, I'm not wondering if I can last 90 minutes.'
David Ginola discovers a hitherto hidden predilection for hard work

Lost for Words

'Gazza's given me three souvenirs – two fat lips and his shirt, which was a nice gesture.'
Wycombe's Steve Brown on his brush with flawed genius

'I'd seen Lee Hughes on my left, so I thought I'd slip the ball into his path. But he decided to stop, making my pass look really awful. I won't make the same mistake again – next time I'll shoot myself.'
James Quinn

'Reaching the play-offs might be a bit much, but aim for the moon and you can reach the stars.'
Peter Beardsley

'Since I came to West Ham people have been trying to find me another club, but it's rubbish.'
Eyal Berkovic denies he's set to join Christian Gross's Tottenham

'Wimbledon are anxious to lose the "Crazy Gang" tag, and they've certainly announced their intentions with the signing of John Hartson.'
Peter Brackley commends the Dons' deranged purchase of the £7.5 million targetman

'You must allow enough time to savour something that is so fantastic. It's like a woman – the longer you wait for one, the more you appreciate it. Every four years is fine.'
Rangers keeper Lionel Charbonnier dismisses plans for a biannual World Cup

'My daughter Olivia came in and I told her Daddy was going to play for England. She began to cry.'
Lee Dixon's bright little girl captures the thoughts of the nation

'I've never wanted to leave. I love the club, the area and
the people and what I'm saying is that I'm here for the
rest of my life, and hopefully after that as well.'
Alan Shearer

'I never read the papers. If you don't want to read the good stuff, don't read the bad ... or should that be the other way round?'
Jamie Redknapp

'When I spoke to the new gaffer he didn't mention relegation once, and it has never crossed my mind that Blackburn will go down ... this club is going places.'
Lee Carsley departs mid-table Derby for greener pastures

'When you think about it, to have gone 10 games unbeaten with this team is unbelievable.'
Steve Coppell appraises the Crystal Palace playing staff

'I dreamt of playing for a club like Manchester United, and now here I am playing for Liverpool.'
Sander Westerveld

'I want to be the Juninho of Scottish football.'
Eyal Berkovic expresses the desire to become Celtic's sole performer

'Leeds is a great club and it's been my home for years, though I still live with my parents in Middlesbrough.'
Jonathon Woodgate

'When people want to go to bed, this is the kind of thing they want to watch just before.'
Brian Moore talks up his soporific late-night chat show on Sky Sports 3

'No manager has ever run on and scored the winning goal yet.'
Dave Bassett is too preoccupied with Forest's relegation scrap to spot Gianluca Vialli's exploits at Chelsea

'Germany are a very difficult team to play ... they had 11 internationals out there today.'
Steve Lomas

'I have played my last match, scored my last goal and elbowed my last opponent. My motivation and my back no longer exist.'
Martin Dahlin

THE WRONG KIND OF SHIRTS '99

'Paulo (Wanchope) was way out of order but I deny any suggestion I ever said he was a poof. I would never use that kind of language even if it was justified.'
Jim Smith is borderline politically correct

'Lombardo speaks much better English than what people realise.'
Mark Goldberg

'I always used to put my right boot on first, and then obviously my right sock.'
Barry Venison

'We never took the game by the scruff of the neck. In the second half, we didn't take them to the cleaners as we would have liked: that would have been the icing on the cake.'
Glenn Hoddle

'She gives the players a shoulder to talk to.'
Neil Webb on Eileen Drewery

'We're in a no-win situation – except that if we win, we go through to the next round.'
Graeme Le Saux ponders a tricky cup-tie at Oxford

'To be second with one game to go – you can't
ask for more.'
Bradford skipper Stuart McCall

'The important thing is he shook hands with us
over the phone.'
Alan Ball

'If you're not prepared to die for your country, you
shouldn't be playing. But I think we have the players
who can go and do that.'
Neville Southall demands absolute commitment

'When you put on the red-and-white shirt you have to
attempt to die in winning the game. When it works out,
it is the best feeling in the world.'
*Sunderland coach Bobby Saxton endorses
Southall's sentiments*

'I do not believe in formations, rather in the systems
you need to make those formations work ... This is all
about communicating with players. You must make
them understand what you're after.'
John Barnes baffles his new Celtic charges

'Warnock, a seasoned crimper and saver ...'
Guardian *misprint*

'When we went to Denmark and when we played
Belarus, I was hanging onto a precipice and my
fingernails were bleeding. And at the end of it we
dug trenches, we had the bayonets out, and
the lads responded.'
Bobby Gould

'I told him to go out and drop a few grenades.'
*Kevin Keegan gets Paul Scholes fired up to face Sweden,
inevitably leading to the player's sending-off*

'If you want me to throw my hat into the ring,
I'll throw in a Stetson.'
*Neville Southall declares a ten-gallon interest in
managing Wales*

'We had good ball circulation but not enough
penetration.'
Arsène Wenger sounds off an idiom

Smartypants

'We are now safe arithmetically, not mathematically.
There's neither algebra nor geometry involved in
the calculations.'
*Tom Hendrie celebrates St Mirren's escape from relegation
with a fine piece of pedantry*

'A player who can conjugate a verb in the first person
singular cannot be part of the squad. He has to
conjugate the verb in the first person plural.'
Brazil coach Wanderley Luxemburgo

'I believe the *Candide* line: cultivate your own garden.
If, of course, someone looks over the wall and says,
"What a lovely garden, perhaps we could get him to do
some gardening for us," then that's a different matter.'
*Roy Hodgson, pre-Blackburn sacking, refuses to rule himself
out of contention for the England job*

'His rich, mellifluous voice is redolent of Sinden and
Gielgud intertwining Shakespeare, Keats, Wordsworth
et al. amid the mud and tears of Accrington Stanley.'
*Former Labour sports spokesman Tom Pendry puts
forward a House of Commons motion celebrating
Stuart Hall's 40 years in broadcasting*

'Victor Hernandez, like an orchestral conductor
directing his troops ...'
Jon Champion

Taking the Mike

'Manchester United have hit the ground running
– albeit with a 3–0 defeat.'
Bob Wilson

'It's not what Ginola does when he's got the ball, it's
what he doesn't do when he hasn't got it.'
Andy Gray

'You just can't underestimate the value he's
been to them.'
*Gaby Yorath devalues Brian Kidd's contribution at
Manchester United*

'A nice little eyebrows from Ekoku, and Euell's nearly
on the end of it.'
Ron Atkinson

'That was only a yard away from being an
inch-perfect pass.'
Murdo MacLeod

'I'll tell you what, zero-zero's a big score.'
Ron Atkinson

'Forest are 1–0 down. This will be their 19th
consecutive game without a win unless they can
conjure an equaliser.'
Alan Green

'It's that old saying, isn't it? A 70 per cent, y'know,
60 per cent fit Ronaldo is better than a 100 per cent,
y'know, somebody else.'
Kevin Keegan

'Fortunately, Paul Scholes' injury wasn't as bad as
we'd hoped for.'
Trevor Brooking

'Smicer has been booked, and he'd better watch his Ps
and Qs – or rather his Zs and Qs in the Czech Republic.'
Gary Bloom

'Flo literally turned Taricco inside-out.'
Trevor Francis

'On comes Koller, a giant in every sense of the
word, er ... 6' 8".'
Gary Bloom

'To a man, every Czech fan is on his or her feet.'
Gary Bloom

'The ageless Dennis Wise, now in his thirties ...'
Martin Tyler

'Charlton are on the crest of a slump.'
Mark Lawrenson

'Er ... Kanu. Tell us about your goal.'
*Tony Gubba decides to wait until the boy Nwankwo is
more established on these shores before pronouncing the
name to camera*

'Now they'll have something else to celebrate in the
city of Parma apart from their delightful hams and
wonderful cheese.'
*Barry Davies gets a little peckish whilst commentating on
the Uefa Cup final*

'Beckham came in like Buddy Holly on the back stick.'
Ron Atkinson

'Now Man United are 2–1 down on aggregate, they are in a better position than when they started the game at 1–1.'
Ron Atkinson

'Villa will probably play a lot worse than this and lose.'
Alan Parry

'That was a needle through the haystack job.'
Clive Allen

'In four years, I'll be 70 years old, and you can never be sure that what you want to come out of your mouth will come out.'
Brian Moore, ruling out a commentating comeback, fails to understand why he was always so cherished

'He (Ronaldo) sent Stam for a cup of tea, two sugars
– and anti-clockwise.'
Mark Lawrenson

Curiosities

'Of the 10 sendings-off, nine have been different
players, so it proves we're unlucky.'
Millwall boss Keith Stevens

'If you think about Scotland in English terms, they are
the West Ham of world football.'
Tony Banks

'To leave Valerenga it had to be Wimbledon or Brazil.
It is not Brazil, so it is Wimbledon.'
Noted eccentric Egil Olsen takes charge of the Dons

'To wake up every morning and know that you are a
footballer is like a very strange and beautiful surprise.
You cannot grow tired of it. Every day I have this
feeling. It is incredible.'
David Ginola

'I managed to complete my objective. The most important thing for us was the fact that Spain didn't manage 14 and break their own record. Then this game would have been talked about for a long time.'
San Marino keeper Frederico Gasperoni reflects on a job well done as his team restricts Spain to a 9–0 victory

'There is plenty of subtlety in this team, only sometimes it doesn't come out.'
Kevin Keegan

'I didn't think we gave the ball away so much as chose the wrong options. It wasn't always bad play, just bad choices.'
Kevin Keegan

'If the nation wants Kevin, the ordinary person wants Kevin and the FA want Kevin, then I will give him to England, no problem. The nation comes first, the glory of the country, and that's the sacrifice we will make at Fulham. Kevin is my gift to the nation.'
Mohammed Al Fayed tries another tack in his continued battle for a British passport

'Every time it strikes me, with all the freshness of
a revelation: going to a football match to watch
a football match is the worst possible way to watch a
football match ... The crowd is a wraparound millipede
of rage and yearning, with the body heat of 180,000
torched armpits, with its ear-hurting roars, and that
incessant whistling like a billion babies joined in one
desperate scream.'

Martin Amis regrets attending the European Cup final

'I have felt the ugly and atavistic lusts of the football fan, and they disquiet me. Nationalism doesn't explain it, though it gave me harsh pleasure to see those Germans with their faces in the mud.'
Martin Amis is touched by beastliness in the company of the lower classes

'I would use an expression used by Pat Jennings – he felt we were mugged a little bit.'
Lawrie McMenemy struggles to come to terms with Northern Ireland's 3–0 reverse at home to Germany

'I want the players to be more crazy and more aggressive. I want spirit among the players – and I've got a spare pair of wellington boots ready. I've seen their jokes and I won't stop it.'
Egil Olsen

'I didn't bite him. The TV showed me gesturing to bite him and obviously everyone has jumped on the bandwagon and said I bit him.'
Dennis Wise discusses the semantics of personal assault, on this occasion on Real Mallorca defender Elena Marcelino

'Me and Joe (Kinnear) are so close, we will carry
on living in the same underpants ... it's been
a unique relationship.'
Sam Hammam

'I'll become another forgotten player, just like
Eric Cantona.'
*Peter Schmeichel announces his impending departure
from Old Trafford*

'Maybe we gave the fans too much last season.
When you get used to caviar, it is difficult to come
back to sausages.'
Arsène Wenger

'Now I find it hard to give the no. 5 shirt to any
Englishman who knows Welsh, because five in Welsh is
"pimp", so he's reluctant to take that shirt.'
Bobby Gould's Welsh language lessons bear fruit

'The kit is dreadful – a blue shirt with green shorts and
green socks. I am very cocky and vain. A keeper needs
charisma and that's impossible wearing green pants.'
Sander Westerveld

'Any team in the world could play against that
Dundee side and drop points.'
Dick Advocaat understates his Rangers team's deficiencies

'Being England coach is like having a shop. If the
people want candy, you put candy on your counter
and you sell more.'
Kevin Keegan

'I feel like going home and dousing myself in four-star petrol. Let's face it, how do you replace John Spencer?'
Motherwell boss (and Spencer's brother-in-law)
Billy Davies overreacts to an apparent breakdown in transfer talks with Everton

'We live in a fantasy. You find yourself watching a flea and thinking how come that flea walks like that? You might stand on the flea then five minutes later a piece of tree falls on you and kills you. I try always to keep my feet on the ground.'
Mohammed Al Fayed

'Our British culture can't play for a draw. We must go for it. It's muck and nettles.'
Bobby Gould

'I was quite surprised with Plymouth's result against Scunthorpe last week, and it was a continuance of what we have seen most of the season. That is, various clubs beating each other.'
Ron Noades

'I know the players I want. It is like I have them in the
fridge waiting to come out.'
Ruud Gullit

'The world is going to end in 2001. I'm considering packing in football at the end of the season and preparing for anything.'
Argentine keeper Carlos Roa turns down a contract extension at Real Mallorca

Pick of the Papers

'It's great that Kevin Keegan has signed for England ...
he understands what the media needs – and what
fans need too. Best of luck, Kev. Everybody's with you
all the way.'
The Sun *gives its full backing to Keegan's appointment as
England coach – for the time being*

'Our Subs Sink Germans'
The Sun *celebrates Manchester United's last-gasp
European Cup final win*

'Parmageddon'
The Daily Record *encapsulates Rangers' latest*
European collapse

'Huge Beast Runs Into Elk'
The Sun *breaks the news of Tomas Brolin's car accident*
back home in Sweden

'You'll Get SFA, Farry'
The Daily Record *dismisses Jim Farry's hopes for a pay-off*
from the Scottish Football Association

'Bermondsey's Top Nonce Sharing Cell With
Shamed Chelsea Coach'
Southwark News *is outraged that south London's finest*
should have to share a cell with Graham Rix

'Batistuta Heads For Goodison'
The Liverpool Echo *reacts over-excitedly to an*
Everton–Fiorentina friendly

Hoddle Twaddle

'I'm not some crackpot who comes out with stupid remarks to cause controversy.'
Glenn Hoddle

'My main concern was to get a quality book out in the sense of what was running more from my mind and my reactions of situations through a World Cup and putting things down on record to a certain degree and having that memory and giving people a bit of insight.'
Glenn Hoddle argues the case for a ghostwriter for his World Cup Diary

'A lot of what Glenn was saying and doing did not impress me. He seemed quite nervous and was whistling a lot – not the sign of a relaxed man.'
Tony Adams

'He's entitled to his opinions, many of which are positive. In a strange way, I think this has brought us closer together.'
Glenn Hoddle

'I've got total respect for the man – not because he's sitting next to me, but because I have.'
Tony Adams

'You and I have been physically given two hands and two legs and half-decent brains. Some people have not been born like that for a reason. The karma is working from another lifetime. What you sow, you reap.'
Glenn Hoddle

'If his theory is correct, he is in for real problems in the next life. He will probably be doomed to come back as Glenn Hoddle.'
Tony Banks

'Thoughts are things. They really are. And if anyone denies that, then they deny the fact that they are living here on this planet. They really are things, and I can see where a healer can help.'
Glenn Hoddle sticks by his singular beliefs

'Hoddle 0 Disabled 1 (Hoddle, o.g.)'
Independent *headline*

'Glenn Hoddle was sacked for his beliefs. Still, 500 years ago you could be burned at the stake for that.'
Arsène Wenger

'I must have been a failed football coach in a previous incarnation.'
David Blunkett

'If she goes, I go.'
Glenn makes the FA's decision a whole lot easier by sticking by Eileen Drewery

'They twisted it all round like I was a freak or he was a bit odd.'
Eileen Drewery

'We choose to come back as we would wish to come back. That may be as a poor man or a rich man and sometimes you come back, if you want to, as a disabled person. That is their choice.'
Eileen Drewery

'Certain newspapers are out to bring him down – that goes with the territory – but on this occasion Hoddle has loaded the revolver and handed it to them butt-end first.'
Guardian

'Too many times he (Hoddle) has used his role to promote his beliefs as a supermarket hippy.'
Gazzetta dello Sport

'Hoddle was stupid and abusive.'
L'Equipe

'People in the West haven't thought like this since the Middle Ages. Hoddle is simply a little mad.'
Corriere dello Sport

THE WRONG KIND OF SHIRTS '99

'Even Graham Taylor left the post with greater dignity
than Hoddle, despite having a root vegetable placed
on his head.'
Express

'I did think at one stage I could do with a beam me up
Scotty job. Just get me out somewhere in a capsule,
floating around in space for a day. It's very, very nice
spinning around in orbit.'
Howard Wilkinson proves an able stand-in for Hoddle

'I haven't been asked, but if I were I would say it was
the wrong time.'
Kevin Keegan begins his prevarications

'Maybe he knows something. He's supposed to be able
to see into the future, isn't he?'
*Terry Venables reacts to Hoddle's claim that he wants the
England job back*

'Terry Venables has as much chance of getting the
England job as Jack the Ripper.'
Graham Kelly

The Romance of the Millennium

'On the Wednesday we played Inter Milan, we went into hospital Thursday and I had him 28 minutes past seven on the Thursday night.'
David Beckham describes the miracle birth of baby Brooklyn

'He loves attention. He doesn't like being put down, he likes to be cuddled all the time.'
Posh Spice describes one of the two most important men in her life

'The apartment is our home, it's not a showpiece ...
it's a cross between a poof's house and a whorehouse.
We're very lucky.'
*Posh rejoices that she and Becks have found a home
where they can just be themselves*

'When I went into the marquee with Victoria earlier, the orchestra was rehearsing *Goodbye* and I got so emotional that I had to take a bike out and cycle round the golf course to get over it.'
Posh's dad, Tony, stays in touch with his emotions – and as far away as possible from the Spice Girls' music

'I will love and look after Victoria and treat her like a princess – which she always wants to be treated like.'
Becks promises to honour and obey

'Victoria Beckham. It does sound a bit like a railway station, doesn't it?'
It dawns on Posh that she shares her first name with a London terminus

'People are always asking me why I always kiss David Beckham. My answer is that I'd usually do much more than that to a six-foot blonde in shorts with legs up to the armpits.'
Becks's best man Gary Neville

'They said they wanted to meet any men who could stay
on top for 90 minutes and still come second.'
*Gary Neville apologises to the Spice Girls that Bayern
Munich couldn't make the ceremony*

THE WRONG KIND OF SHIRTS
Mark Reynolds

Alex Ferguson makes a ridiculous claim that his
players can't see each other in their grey strip as
they lose at Southampton, and a series is born.
But who has the last laugh? Fergie out-psyches
Kevin Keegan and claims the championship;
Scotland are defeated by England at Euro '96;
while in the semi-final Wembley tingles with
anticipation as Gareth Southgate steps up to
take the deciding penalty against the Germans.

1 85702 602 0 £3.99

THE WRONG KIND OF SHIRTS 2
Mark Reynolds

Another year, another unlikely defeat for
Manchester United at Southampton. Eric says
adieu; Arsène takes the reins at Highbury and
learns the art of bickering; while Middlesbrough's
foreign stars jump ship as Bryan Robson's team
are relegated on a technicality.

1 85702 760 4 £3.99

THE WRONG KIND OF SHIRTS '98
Mark Reynolds

Manchester United end the season empty-handed!
More amazingly, a team managed by Alan Ball
finishes comfortably clear of the relegation zone.
And at France '98, Mary Poppins leads the line
for England, David Batty has a Southgate moment
against Argentina, and Arsenal win the World Cup.

1 85702 873 2 £3.99

FOOTBALL IN SUN AND SHADOW
Eduardo Galeano

To the pure football fan, even winning and losing is of secondary importance to those moments when a glimpse is afforded of footballing perfection – made more perfect still by the long, unpredictable, tragicomic hours spent waiting and watching for the miraculous event to unfold. Such instants of exultation and despair are brilliantly recounted in this parade of all shades of international football.

'A global history with the poetic flair of a Pelé free kick.' *The Face*

1 85702 711 6   £6.99

THE GOALKEEPER'S HISTORY OF BRITAIN
Peter Chapman

A captivating mixture of allusive anecdote and observation that charts the changing nature of Britain and the country's peculiar visceral attachment to its goalkeepers. Chapman's search takes him from Hackney Marshes to the North Cape, from the dustmen's depots of Finsbury to his own selection for a Brazil XI, led by Rivelino, that had forgotten to include a goalkeeper.

'Entertaining, inventive ... perceptive and illuminating. Great book.' *When Saturday Comes*

1 84115 009 6   Hardback   £16.99

All Fourth Estate books are available from your local bookshop,
or can be ordered direct (FREE UK p&p) from:

Fourth Estate, Book Service By Post, PO Box 29,
Douglas, I-O-M, IM99 1BQ

Credit cards accepted.

Tel: 01624 836000   Fax: 01624 670923

Or visit the Fourth Estate website at:
www.4thestate.co.uk

*Prices are correct at time of going to press, but may be subject to
change. Please state when ordering if you do **not** wish to receive
further information about Fourth Estate titles.*